GOING OUT ON A LIMERICK FOR DOGS AND CATS 50/50

AUTHOR DARYL L. OLSON
ARTIST NICOLE FUHRMANN-DERUYCK

U.S. $18.00/CAN. $27.00

Printed in the United States of America

Library of Congress Cataloging-in-Publication Data.

Going Out On A Limerick for Dogs And Cats 50/50
By Daryl Olson.

ISBN: 09710147-2-8

10 9 8 7 6 5 4 3 2 1

Daryl Olson Communications, St. Paul, MN
is the sole owner, producer, and distributor of
Going Out On A Limerick for Dogs And Cats 50/50.

Dedication

I dedicate this book to the professional people everywhere who have devoted their life's work to making the world a better place for dogs and cats. I refer to veterinarians and other pet health care people who on a daily basis care for the physical well being of these animals. I have paced the floor or at least shared the anxiety with pet owners who have suffered as they wait for good news after an operation on their little four-footed friends. I refer to dedicated people who work long hours at humane societies and animal rescue services and animal adoption services trying to get eager cats and dogs into good homes, where people will take proper care of them. I refer to the scientists and research people who spend their time trying to expand the quality of life for these pets and other animals. I refer to professional organizations that publish books and magazines for cat and dog lovers, written and pictorial splashes of happiness that ease the heavy burdens the sometimes harsh real world imposes upon us. I refer to the numerous cartoonists who feature family members from Garfield to Marmaduke, who truly are the tails that wag their masters, so we can all laugh as we swap our favorite incidents and enjoy their antics together. I refer to any and all people I've forgotten to mention, whose spirit and dedication to our sniffy snurfy friends make their lives better, and conversely make our own lives happier.

Daryl L.Olson

Introduction

I have been accused of being an animal lover. When I think about it, I guess this accusation is true. When I was about two years old, I fell in love with animals of all sorts, as my mother would read to me from various animal books replete with pictures, and I savored this experience. My mother was very thorough, as she included books of birds and marine life and domestic animals and wild animals in her readings. When she came to the books which featured the world's big cats, my interest in animals took a significant and permanent leap upward. Then I truly fell in love with these magnificent creatures, so graceful and powerful and unique, and I especially became enamored with the tiger, which I considered the most graceful and beautiful creature on earth. From that point on, I adorned my room (by request, of course) with various pictures and replicas of tigers in various poses. Even today, my bedroom features several tiger pictures, with a lynx and a pair of lions thrown in for good measure.

Over my teaching tenure of more than two decades, I taught twenty-four different speech courses and twenty-four different English courses, including several courses involving poetry and writing poetry. Gradually the idea for this book fleshed out and took shape. The limerick is a unique poetic form, designed to get attention, arouse interest, provide information, make social commentary, simulate feelings, and provide humor, all within five lines. Obviously, no limerick should be expected to do all of the above at once, but various combinations thereof, all of which are included numerous times in this book. Since this book is partially intended for the enjoyment of children, as well as for adults, of course, I'm aware of the impact poetry has upon children, an advantage utilized successfully by Dr. Seuss and hundreds of writers previously. Combine a memorable poetic form with beautiful human-produced drawings by my talented artist, and we have, I hope, the foundation for a book that can be a huge enjoyment for readers of all ages.

Finally, I decided to go out on a limerick for dogs and cats to appeal to the sixty million dog or cat or dog/cat owners in the United States alone. I had to split the book between dogs and cats exactly fifty-fifty, since I surely did not want conflict because there were one or two more dogs or cats included! Good grief, who could afford the controversy that might ensue if either dogs or cats seemed to be favored in this book! As far as the choice of which dogs and cats got included, I perused two dozen books to try to determine which breeds were most popular and representative and drawable. Every writer and book has to know its limitations. If I left out your favorite cat or dog, all I can say is, I'm sorry, better luck next time perhaps. With regard to writing the limericks for dogs versus cats, doing the cat limericks was far more difficult and challenging. That's true because dogs provide an infinite variety with regard to size and appearance and especially function. Cats are supposed to mostly lie around, stretch, purr, and keep their owners in line. So for the cat limericks, I had to read several histories of the various breeds to provide a more historical and factual and informative approach to make them unique. My own cat, Palsy, was especially helpful and supportive in this whole venture, which made my task easier.

Daryl L. Olson

Table of Contents

Preface

A DOG'S PRAYER

Treat me kindly, my beloved master, for no heart in all the world is more grateful for kindness than the loving heart of mine.

Do not break my spirit with a stick, for though I should lick your hand between the blows, your patience and understanding will more quickly teach me the things you would have me do.

Speak to me often, for your voice is the world's sweetest music, as you must know by the fierce wagging of my tail when your footstep falls upon my waiting ear.

When it is cold and wet, please take me inside, for I am now a domesticated animal, no longer used to bitter elements. And I ask no greater glory than the privilege of sitting at your feet beside the hearth. Though you had no home, I would rather follow you through ice and snow than rest upon the softest pillow in the warmest home in all the land, for you are my god and I am your devoted worshipper.

Keep my pan filled with fresh water, for although I should not reproach you were it dry, I can not tell you when I suffer thirst. Feed me clean food, that I may stay well, to romp and play and do your bidding, to walk by your side, and stand ready, willing and able to protect you with my life should your life be in danger.

And, beloved master, should the great Master see fit to deprive me of my health or sight, do not turn me away from you. Rather hold me gently in your arms as skilled hands grant me the merciful boon of eternal rest – and I will leave you knowing with the last breath I draw, my fate was ever safest in your hands.

By Beth Norman Harris

A CAT'S PRAYER

Perhaps you think I sleep too much, my dear kind master, but you must know that I am just basking in the comfort and safety of your protective care. Besides, sometimes my cat naps are only a ruse to watch you through half closed lids as you read or write or do your chores, and if you put your ear to my body, you can hear that soft rattle of appreciation and love for you.

Once in awhile I pretend to be standoffish, but this too is only a ploy to make you reach for me or stroke my fur, so I can reassure myself that I am your cat and that you are my human. Even when I'm trying to be coy, my tail gives me away, curled toward you, and I'll give you nose or chin kisses if you put your face close to mine.

I love it when you play with me, when we both pretend that a simple cord or ribbon is a deadly enemy that must be neutralized by my chewy mouth and flying paws. And I know too that these fantasy battles help to reactivate the beauty of your imagination, a vital element that too many adults forsake when they leave their childhood behind. For I am but a whiskered four-pawed extension of your precious childhood, blessed with that unique purr that makes us both so happy, because we know it is the sound that transcends our mortal coils, yours and mine, dear master.

By Palsy Olson

Title Page Revisited

Going Out On a Limerick For Dogs And Cats 50/50

Author Daryl L. Olson
Artist Nicole Fuhrmann-DeRuyck

The Afghan Hound

They're the movie stars of the dog world

With lovely fur coats and their eyelashes curled

If you ask for an autograph

They might smile but they won't laugh

They want their admirers plural

Fifi

The Airedale Terrier

He's the largest of all terriers the Airedale

His good snuffer nose lets him follow a trail

A straight tail and hang-a-down ears

A versatile hunter without any fears

If he keeps his goatee trimmed he'll prevail

BARBER
Shop

The Alaskan Malamute

They've pulled thousands of sleds throughout history

They're so hardy and strong that's no mystery

I think they secretly yearn

For that time it's their turn

To enjoy a sled ride straight or twisty

The Basset Hound

Most people smile when they observe the Basset Hound

With its sad face and floppy ears that nearly touch the ground

Hearing this dog's sonorous baying

I think he's probably saying

If you think you've had a bad day just stick around

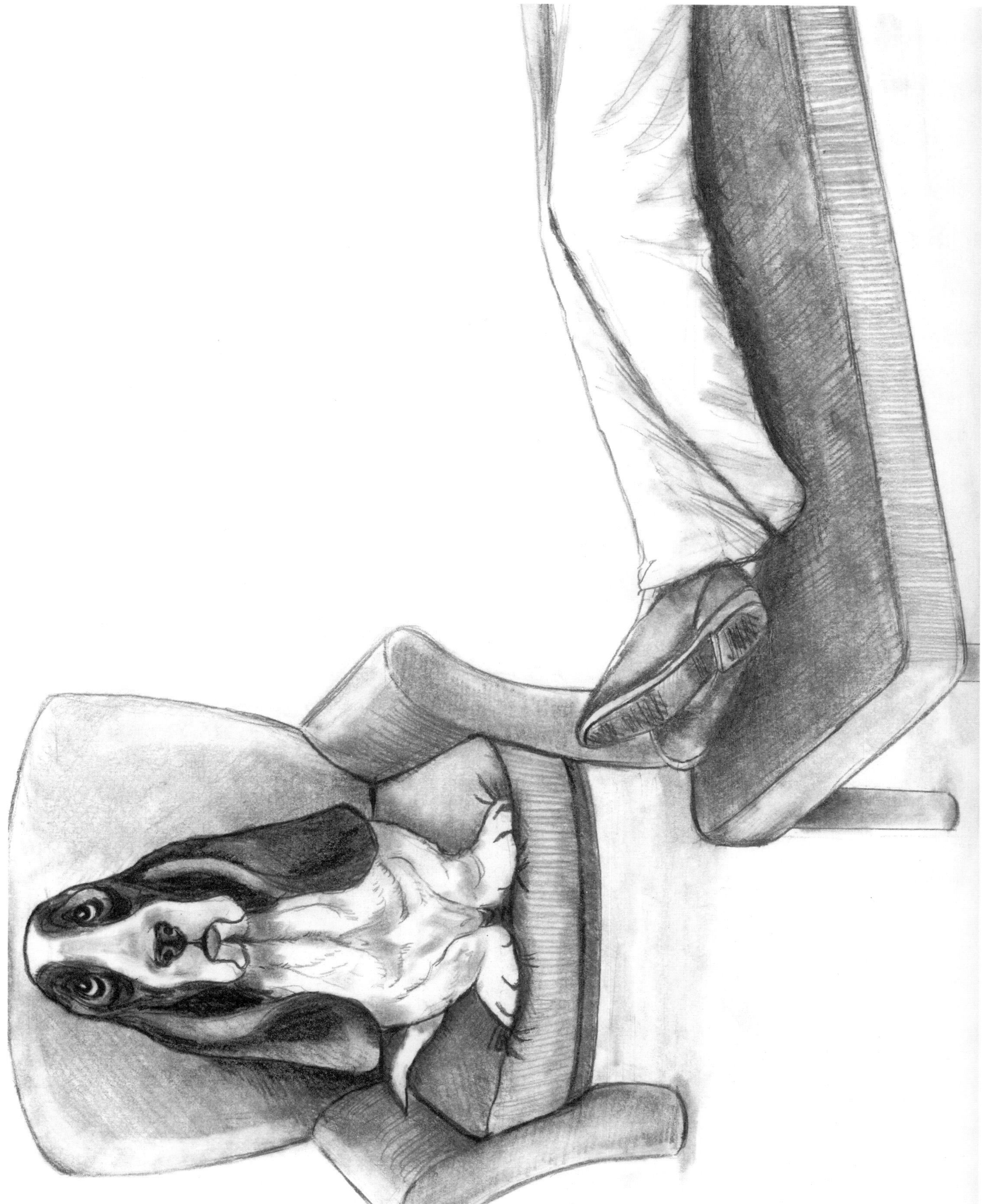

The Bloodhound

The Bloodhound has an incredible nose

His nose knows where a criminal goes

He is always in fine form

And can snuff up a storm

His nose helps to keep crooks on their toes

The Boxer

Despite its name this fine dog's not a fighter

Not a child nipper nor a mail person biter

He might sniff you or snuff you

But won't likely rebuff you

A few pats make relationships tighter

US MAIL
FIDO
101 Dog Lane
Dogtown, U.S.A.

The Bulldog

Taurus is their sign astrological

They're smart but not pedagogical

They're Great Britain's national symbol

Once used to bait bulls strong but nimble

A bit stubborn but mostly they're logical

TAURUS DAILY
HOROSCOPE
MON. 20th
KICK BACK TODAY
AND GET
SOME REST

The Chihuahua

The world's smallest dog can be hidden

In places that would seem to be forbidden

Like a fine lady's purse

And when she finds him what's worse

He might refuse to do what he is bidden

The Chow Chow

This heavy coated dog has been cast

As both a sleigh and guard dog in the past

But I have the illusion

He must have some confusion

Because his first name is the same as his last

The Collie

The Collie dog is very classy

Whether it's a lad or a lassie

It will play with the children

And won't eat your philodendron

And will seldom get nippy or sassy

The Coonhound

These dogs just love hunting raccoons

And they'll bay like they're seeing two moons

You'll probably not see

One barking up the wrong tree

Nor ever hear them bark out of tune

The Dachshund

The Dachshund is long low and lean

Look down or he'll pass you unseen

These dogs look just a tetch

Like they forget to unstretch

But they won't get caught leaving the scene

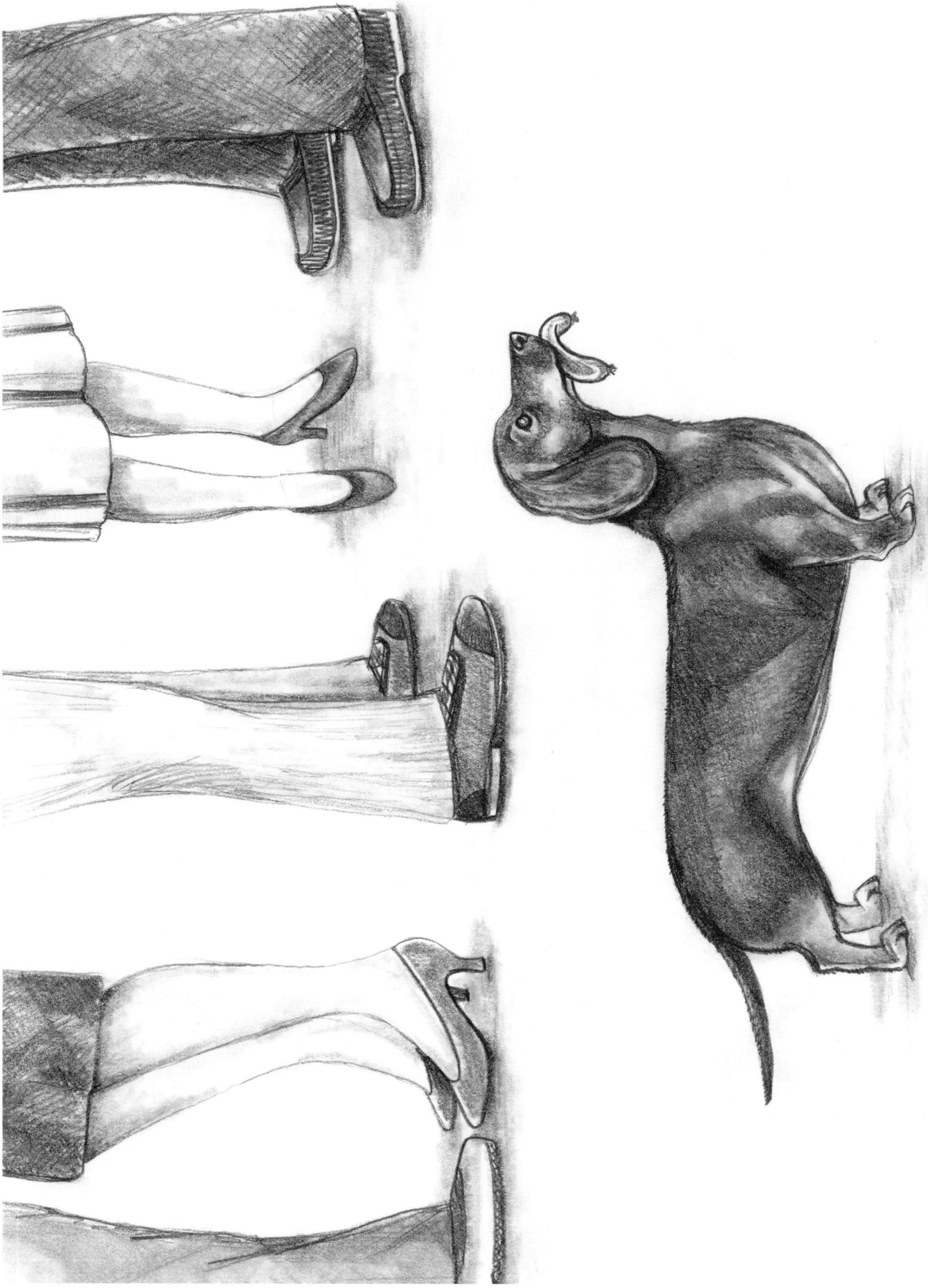

The Dalmatian

On firetrucks these fine dogs like to hover

They're on tap until the crises is over

Although it hardly seems fair

They have a recurring nightmare

About being sprayed with a strong spot remover

SPOT
REMOVER

The Deerhound

About the Deerhound I don't have much to say

Except it's probably having a bad hair day

And the deer that they are after

Are probably too weak from laughter

To concentrate upon getting away

The Doberman

As guard dogs they are truly awesome

You're better off if you don't cross 'em

Just drive by but don't park

Their bite is worse than their bark

Thank goodness their masters can boss 'em

FORT KNOX

The English Cocker Spaniel

The spaniel has been around for fifteen hundred years

Which may or may not explain why they have such long ears

These cocker boys have such wavy fur coats

We'd never mistake them for sheep or for goats

And they are well thought of by their peers

MOST
POPULAR

The English Pointer

This hunting dog many hunters anoint

Bragging it up 'till its nose is out of joint

Yet while hunting they relish

You'd think being English

They'd know that it's impolite to point

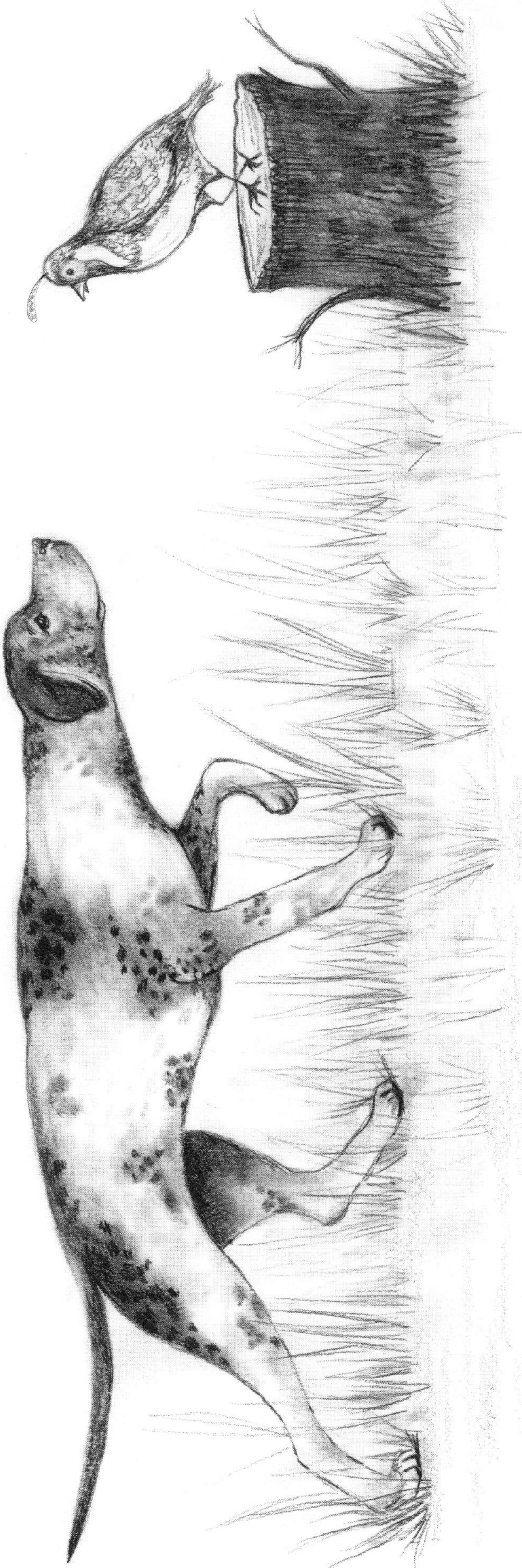

The English Springer Spaniel

This dog's freckled face is quite charming

It looks so happy it's almost disarming

It has long wavy ears

Has no tears or no fears

And can even help out if you're farming

The German Shepherd

A seeing-eye dog who will always stay near

Or a police dog who performs without fear

A conversation sparker

This talented woofybarker

Could well be voted dog of the year

The Golden Retriever

This dog is so good natured and loyal

Its owners feel well loved almost royal

It will not only lick your hand

It will probably strike up the band

More than kind their masters they spoil

The Great Dane

The Great Dane is a very good sport

Fortunately he's the affable sort

Most dogs think that it's fair

To steal your favorite chair

This dog can take up your whole davenport

The Great Pyrenees

This dog is so big it could eat you

But instead will just sniff you and greet you

But for their massive fur coat

A live in groomer gets my vote

Or all that hair will most likely defeat you

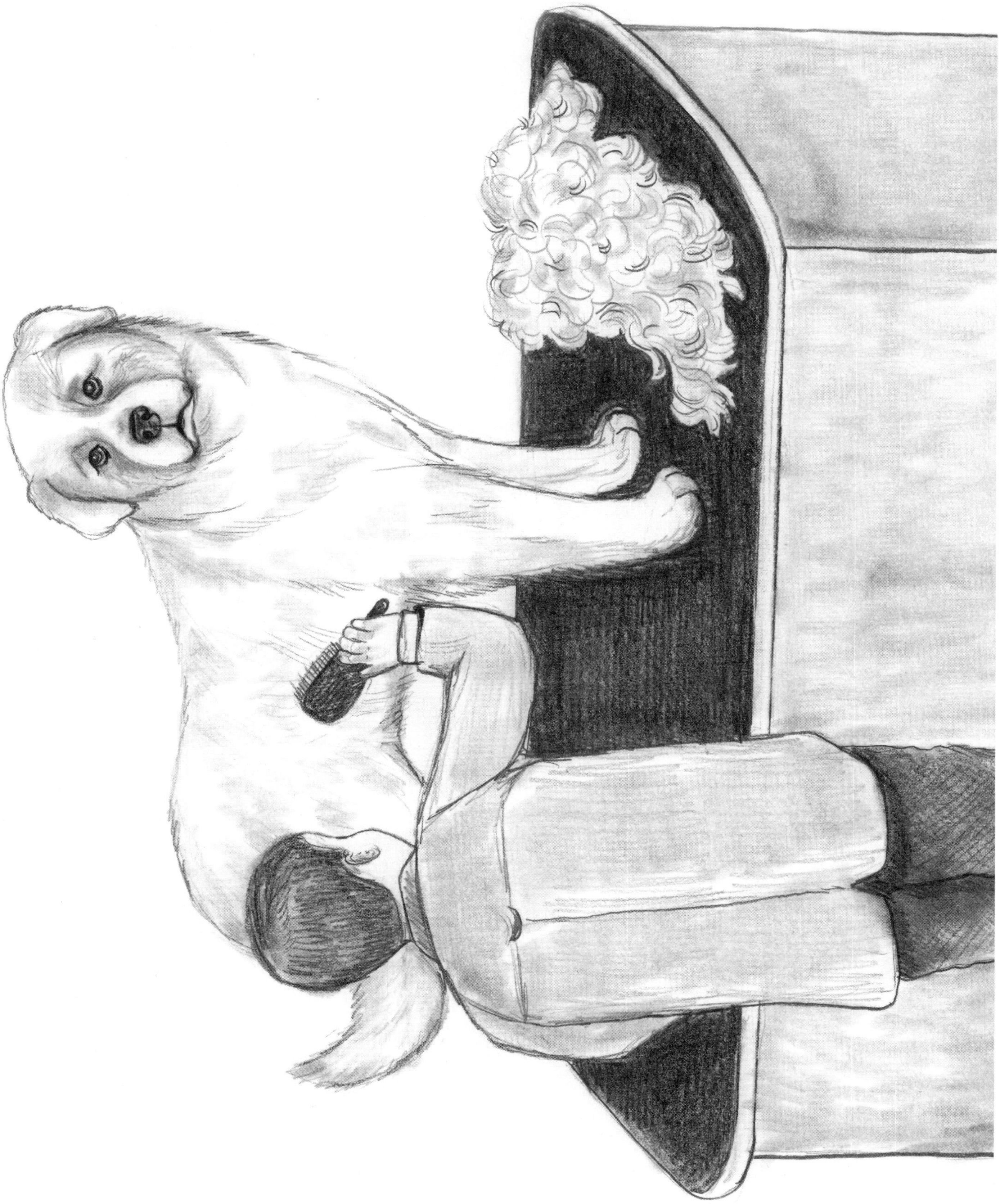

The Greyhound

Greyhounds will chase a mechanical rabbit

They'd like to catch up to one and just grab it

They've never caught one yet

So it's a pretty good bet

If they could swear they'd at least say dagnabit

5
1
2

The Irish Wolfhound

This dog once killed every wolf in Ireland

He was known as a wolf killing firebrand

He's gentle and kind to his master

Who will not court disaster

A wolf costume for Halloween could get out of hand

The Jack Russell Terrier

I just wonder what a person has to do

To have a terrier named after you

I think this fellow Jack Russell

Had political muscle

Enough to tell the dog namers what to do

NAME CHART
JABERWOCKY TERRIER
JACK RUSSELL TERRIER
JADED TERRIER
JAGGED TERRIER

The Komondor

This dog has an incredible hairstyle

Odd enough to make a dreadlocker smile

A cost-conscious consumer

Would hate paying their groomer

To groom one would probably take awhile

GROOMING
DONE IN ONE HOUR
WEEK!

The Labrador Retriever

These good-looking good-natured retrievers

Have made their various masters believers

Their demeanor is pleasant

They'll fetch a duck or a pheasant

They qualify as tension relievers

The Maltese

Perhaps eight hundred years ago in Crete

A Maltase got embarrassed by dirty feet

And though those ancestors made recompense

Nobody has seen their feet since

They're just trying to keep being discreet

The Newfoundland

This thick-coated kind gentle giant

Is easy to train and quite reliant

They'll listen to you talk

Or take the kids for a walk

It's good when big dogs are so pliant

The Old English Sheepdog

These fluffy cuddly-looking dogs learn

To tend sheep thus their keep they can earn

Visual contact seems fleeting

So they must hear the bleeting

To be able to make a ewe turn

The Pekingese

This dog is very little but mighty

A threat to its master makes it bitey

With a light coat and dark face

It never seems of place

And it seldom acts flippant or flighty

The Pomeranian

If you hear this tiny dog’s loud yap yippings

You’d swear he’d written all his own press clippings

About a watchdog deluxe

But he doesn’t just scare ducks

But in his mind mighty lions he's ripping

The Pug

He's not blessed with an attractive mug

In fact he's quite homely the pug

He snores and grunts in addition

A warm heart belies his condition

He could probably use a good hug

The Rhodesian Ridgeback

Once a lion hunting dog from Rhodesia

This dog is now most happy to please ya

A coarse haired strip on their back

Earned them the odd name the Ridgeback

His tail is wagging as soon says he sees ya

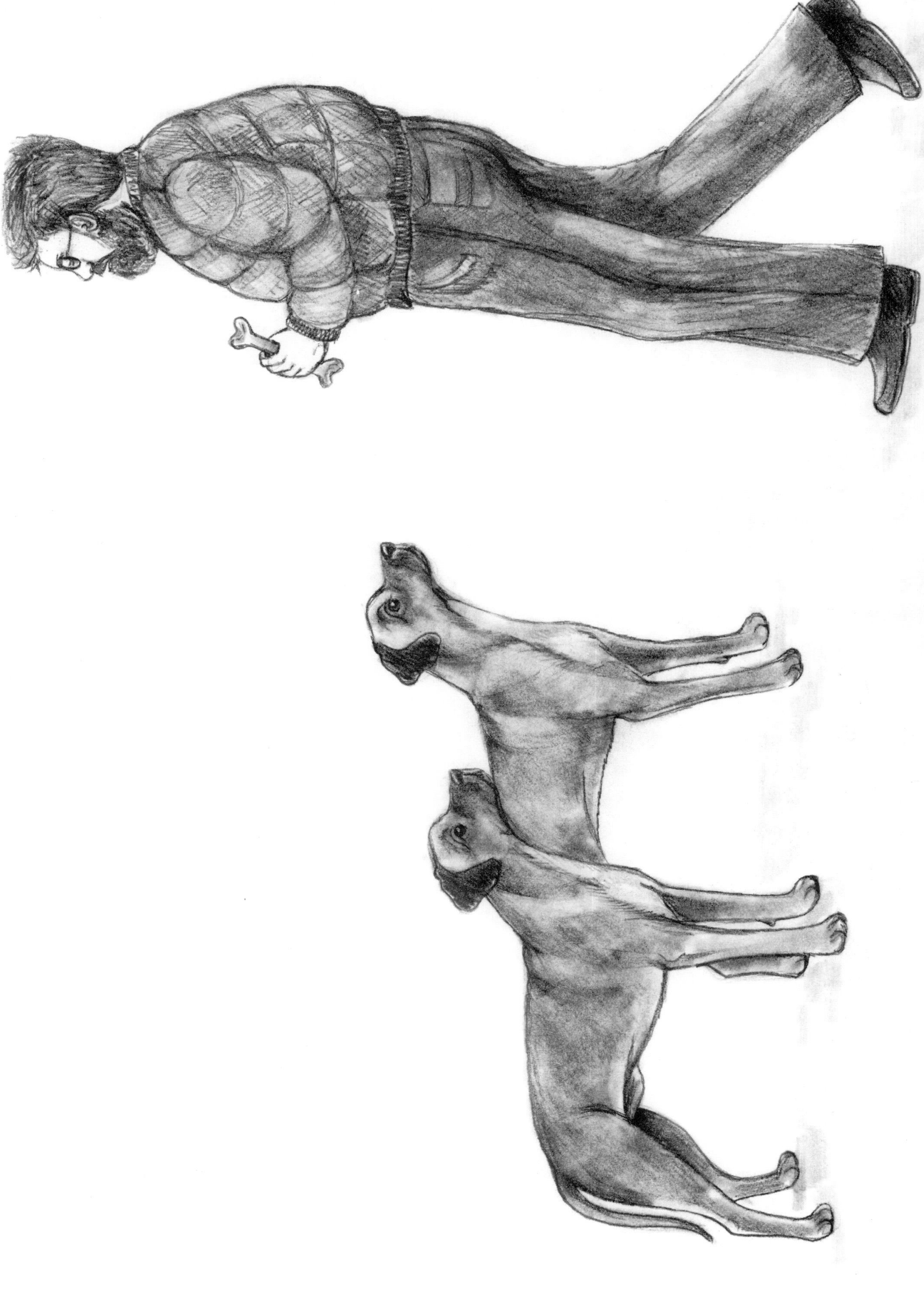

The Russian Sheepdog

This dog's seen three centuries of Russian history

From the Czars to present intrigue and mystery

He'd rather mind his own business and keep

His life nonpolitical and watch sheep

If he knows too much his life can become history

PRAVADA
AND THE
COMMUNIST
PARTY

The Saint Bernard

The enormous but gentle St. Bernard

Could probably cover half your front yard

He can bring lost stragglers brandy

For small children's rides he's dandy

To feed him takes a gold credit card

The Schnauzer

Of German extraction is the Schnauzer

He'd resent being called Bowser

He'd eat wieners and sauerkraut

And enjoy it no doubt

He's not shy but he's not a carouser

A
Dog's Life

The Scottish Terrier

They make fine little dogs residential

Their attitude makes them feel presidential

They can run fetch or push

Or hide behind a bush

These Scotties have an impressive credential

The Shetland Sheepdog

Often dubbed as a collie that's been downsized

This popular dog doesn't mind being revised

Commonly known as the Sheltie

He likes to dwell on what can be

And he doesn't mind being advised

GOOD
DOG
ETIQUETTE
GOOD DOG ETIQUETTE

The Siberian Husky

With their precision sled-pulling deployment

Their hard working nature prompts enjoyment

In a world where too many just get by

You can count on these fine huskies to try

You'll never find them collecting unemployment

The Skye Terrier

This dog appears to be going incognito

But he actually has a healthy libido

A favorite of Queen Victoria

He enjoyed aristocratic euphoria

The Skye's the limit just don't name him Fido

SIR
EDWARD
II

The Toy Poodle

This little fellow's fur attire is hilarious

With fur muffs on his legs and places precarious

They're the national dog of France

So no wonder they'll prance

Poodles are also nimble and dexterous

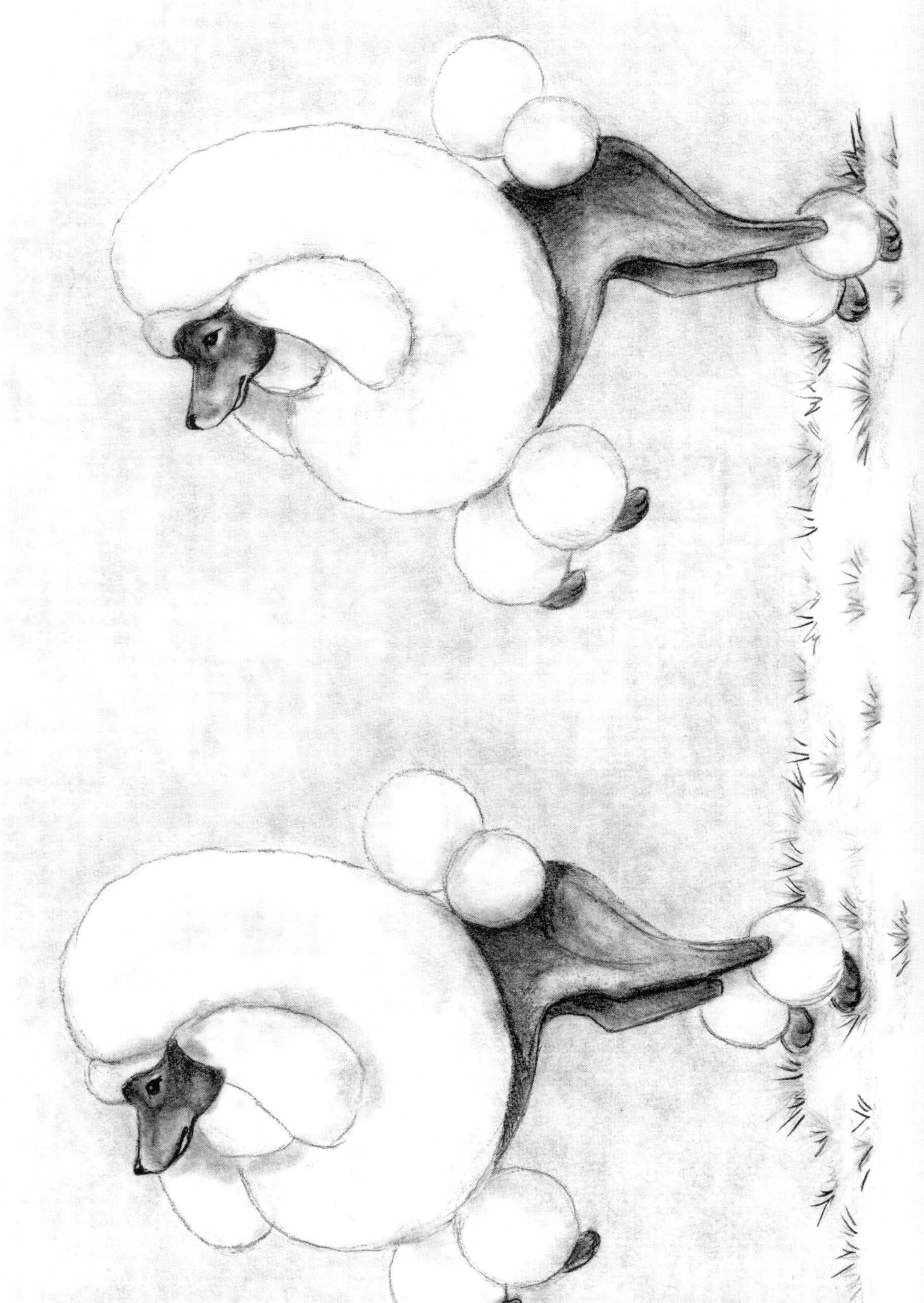

The Weimaraner

This handsome dog is in perfect condition

With a long storied and noble tradition

Once painted by Van Dyke

This canine's easy to like

So he's unlikely to lose his position

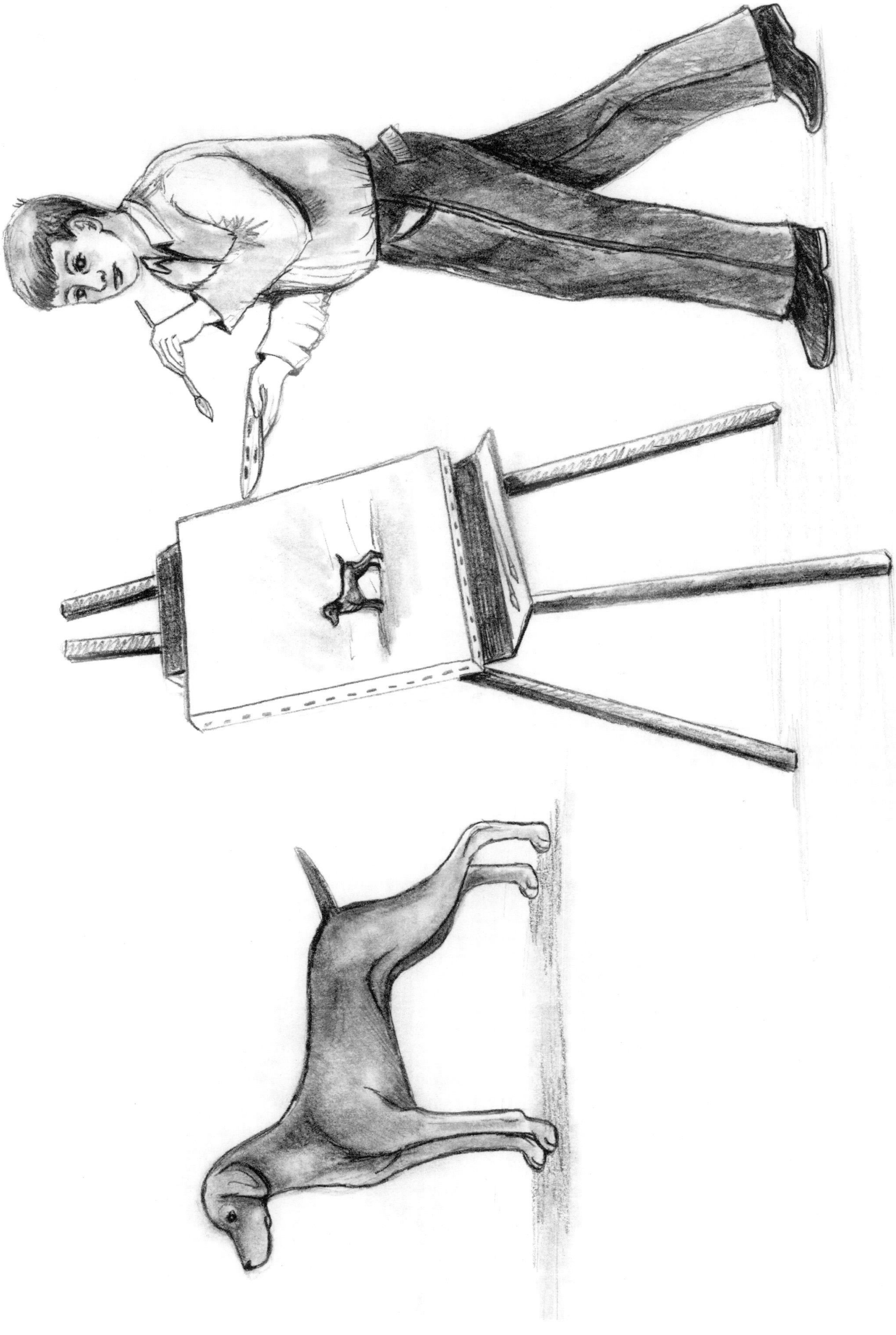

The Welsh Terrier

This small terrier is comical and eager to please

It will rest its chin whiskers on your knees

They have short erect tails

Their ancestors lived in Wales

They are probably expecting a good squeeze

The Whippet

Once nicknamed the Lancashire racehorse

This dog enjoys fast running of course

They're so fast for all you know

They might outrace their shadow

And meet themselves coming back from the source

START

The Yorkshire Terrier

This little doggy just loves to play house

And though its tiny mistress might grouse

At being dressed lacy and frilly

They might both feel somewhat silly

What darling photos mom can show to her spouse

The Beagle

These dogs love to wander and explore

So beware of an unattended open door

The smallest of hounds with ears droopy

They could even be called snoopy

Name tags have been essential many times before

BONNIE
CLYDE
LULU

The Foxhound

The Foxhound is a baying fox finder

Who'll chase foxes but to humans they're kinder

The entire pack will rally so

They can hear horseman yell tallyho

Hunting can be a cross species binder

The Irish Setter

The Irish Setter looks expressive and regal

A red haired and aloof canine eagle

This dog is quite beautiful

At times more excitable than dutiful

The pups are almost too cute to be legal

Wire Fox Terrier

Once known as the chorus girl of the dog world

This dapper dog darling keeps its chin whiskers curled

With more best-in-show prizes

Than any other dog comprises

No wonder they can't wait until their banner is unfurled

GRAND
CHAMPION
WIRE FOX TERRIER

Burmese Cat

In the Thai Cat Book that covered four hundred years

These cats were deemed sacred from their tails to their ears

Described as beautiful with a color like copper

The Burmese is an actual historical showstopper

This world recognized breed now inspires many cheers

The Japanese Bobtail Longhair Cat

This pleasant sweet cat will likely prevail

Even though its name is twice as long as its tail

With Calico markings and a soft gentle face

Its best intentions are always in place

So this cat's bond with its humans won't fail

The Somali Cat

Basically a long-haired Abyssinian cat version

This cat seeks compliance not diversion

The red fox cat it's been called

Its admirers are enthralled

With this champion pussy cat conversion

The Turkish Van Cat

This lovely cat is a native of Van Turkey

It's soft-voiced and sociable not lurky

While white fur might prevail

With its auburn face and tail

It's attitude is very lively and perky

The Abyssinian Cat

Its orange brown ticked coat makes it very unique

It asserts its independence every day of the week

It came from Abyssinia now known as Ethiopia

Its almond-shaped eyes seldom suffer from myopia

This intelligent pussy has plenty of cheek

ABYSSINIAN
Admiration Society
CHARTER MEMBER

The American Bobtail Cat

This attractive cat likely gives daily thanks

He's short half a tail but compared to the Manx

He can still swish his tail and wave it around

Much better than having no tail to be found

For personality the Bobtail gets high ranks

The American Curl Cat

His cat is identified by the way its ears curl

An infrequent gene mutation will case them to furl

Kittens are born with straight ears which curl up then relax

The adult cats remain kittenish and playful to the max

Perhaps uptight adult humans should give this gene a whirl

The American Shorthair Cat

This cat is truly patriotic American in manner

They might join in singing the Star Spangled Banner

These cats were deployed to control pests on the Mayflower

As superior mousers they've enjoyed their best hour

They'd top the list of any pest control planner

BEWARE:
CAT ON
PATROL

The Angora Cat

A traditional blue-eyed white cat with soft fur

Indiscriminate breeding had it close to extinction for sure

Thanks to the Angora Breed Club and the Ankara Zoo

They resurrected the breed from oblivian it's true

These delicate beauties again have reason to purr

Saving
the
ANGORA

The Balinese Cat

A slim long-haired blonde version of the Siamese cat

This fashion model of the cat world knows where it's at

The magazine Speaking Balinese was launched by breeders

It had plenty of style but not too many readers

The mag was Pulitzer Prize quality from where this cat sat

Speaking
BALINESE
1

The Bengal Cat

With wild cat ancestry and distinct leopard spots

These cats were for rich folks and not for have nots

Until recently Bengal cats cost thousands of dollars

Bankers could afford them but not likely scholars

Time payments would help some but not lots

The Birman Cat

Although they look like a long-haired Siamese

This breed's origin is really Burmese

Their beauty seldom has flaws

And they all have white paws

These sweet creatures are eager to please

The British Blue Cat

Unlike the Russian Blue this cat meows in English

But the cat world usually overcomes their linguistics

When they want to be fed all cats speak esperanto

To heck with your technique just give them food pronto

Cats are much more concerned with results than statistics

The Burmilla Cat

This cat came from a Chinchilla and Burmese accidental mating

Which surprised everyone because they hadn't been dating

The resulting cat was essentially a silver Burmese

With elegant features from it tail to its knees

Mother Nature's agenda is sometimes her own if we please

TODAY
Create the
BURMILLA
Cat Breed

The California Spangled Cat

Developed in a breeding program carefully planned

Kittens a price in the thousands command

Introduced to the world through the Nieman Marcus Catalog

This spotted high IQ beauty's becoming a demigod

Supply can't begin to keep up with demand

GIVE
The
PERFECT
Gift
ASK ABOUT
LOAN OPTIONS

The Chartreux Cat

Known for its thick blue-grey coat and orange eyes

A rare breed that's considered a prize

Once the Monastery Cat of the Carthusian Order

Whether it really lived there or was only a border

Its meow prayers still elicit deep sighs

The Cornish Rex Cat

Sometimes called the poodle cat for its wavy rumpled coat

It's cold sensitive but it still gets a strong vote

As one of the feline world's best leapers

After watching one jump you might check your peepers

The chance it has hidden wings is pretty remote

CAT

The Coupari Cat

This long-haired version of the cat Scottish Fold

Has big eyes like brown diamonds and a heart filled with gold

A soft name like Palsy would surely seem fitting

He can be your best pal and wherever you're sitting

He'll keep both your heart and your hands from the cold

The Cymric Cat

This cat is really just a Manx with long hair

Perhaps trying to cover up for a tail that's not there

If that's true I'd like to offer some advice

We all have some weak qualities and some that are nice

And this cat has many good points to share

The Devon Rex Cat

A thin-coated furred cat with curly whiskers and eyebrows

It's unusual enough to appeal to commoners or highbrows

Its wags it tail when it's happy

It will fetch and even follow so snappy

But at least it doesn't bark it just me-ows

The Egyptian Mau Cat

This unique striped or spotted breed was elected

To represent the Ancient Pharaoh's special feline selected

Like those painted on walls second millennium B.C.

In Egypt four thousand years before you and me

But the modern cat doesn't know what the ancients erected

The Exotic Shorthair Cat

A short-haired version of the Persian but easier to maintain

Owners enjoy this purr meister minus the energy drain

While this cat might be sometimes called pleasingly plump

It maintains its dignity and can't be labeled a frump

And what's more it's intelligent and easy to train

ATKINS
DIET

The Havana Brown Cat

This elegant brown cat is like a custom made car

Its name was inspired by the color of a Havana cigar

It has a small sweet face with prominent ears

That make certain our fine feline hears

All compliments whether from near or afar

THIS JUST IN- THE HAVANA BROWN CAT HAS JUST BEEN SELECTED...

The Himalayan Cat

This cat draws its ancestry from Siamese and Persian

With perhaps the best characteristics of each version

From the Persian a quiet voice and more controlled manner

From the Siamese it enterprises a more vigorous banner

Sometimes we can gain from immersion

Nothing VENTURED Nothing GAINED
CONTROL IS THE KEY

The Javanese Cat

This cat is long-haired which excludes classification as Siamese

And lacks color points which excludes being Balinese

This elegant cat has plenty of good points of its own

But sometimes what we aren't is how we are known

And cats and humans need to shake the same trees

FAMiLY
TREE

The Korat Cat

This handsome grey cat came from Thailand's aristocracy

It took hundreds of years to reach my land's registry

They were traditional wedding gifts to bring brides good luck

A highly prized cat that's always been high buck

It's the kind of proud cat that could help rule a monarchy

The La Perm Cat

Perhaps no cat ever looked more like its name

Than this curly-coated tabby grand dame

Like it just walked out of a beauty salon

Wearing a permed coat of loose ringlets right on

But from Dalles La Perm Oregon it came

FEFE LA PERM
Beauty
Parlor

The Maine Coon Cat

The first truly American show cat to ever prevail

This cat could get a back ache just carrying its tail

From Maine to other countries they've been exported

They're better known than Maine lobster it's been reported

These popular cats get a lot of fan mail

The Manx Cat

This pedigree cat has got reason to wail

With normal feline features but missing a tail

Children can't pull its tail without one to pull

So the Manx is optimistic its cup is half full

And so we come to the end of this tale

The Munchkin Cat

With a name handle like Munchkin what can we expect

Criticized for too-short legs like a feline derelict

But even for short legs advantages can be found

Besides that all its legs go clear to the ground

Like the accepted Dachshund dog it's slowly earning respect

The Nebulung Cat

An American bred long-haired version of the Russian Blue

Its double coat is so fluffy it doesn't know what to do

It could wear out three tongues trying to lick itself clean

Thank goodness when groomers appear on the scene

This fluff ball might employ a whole crew

The Norwegian Forest Cat

Kind agile bold and not a bit standoffy

This huge cat has a ruff that's all puffy

But because it's Norwegian

From the forests of that region

It would probably like a good cup of coffee

The Ocicat

This breed has retained some of the wild cat's look

But its temperament is domestic right out of the book

It's been described as a purr wrapped in polka dots

Breeders utilized the kittens that had the most spots

This cat's so domestic it might even learn to cook

The Oriental Shorthair Cat

Its background is Siamese but he's procured a new coat

This good looking tabby's ancestry seems almost remote

With more than a dozen multi-colored cousins

They like to walk with a leash which has caused buzzings

He'll get both the cat and the dog lover's vote

The Peke-Faced Cat

This cat strongly resembles the Pekinese doggy indeed

With a flat face like it hit a brick wall running full speed

Like many humans from sinus problems it often suffers

But these problems are off set by the friendship it offers

Because we strongly value a good friend in need

The Persian Cat

The glamorous woolly coated Persian

Can be considered a maximum upkeep version

Of a proud feline queen

Whose long hair must be kept clean

It had better never develop brush/comb aversion

The Ragdoll Cat

When held it goes limp like a floppy ragdoll

With personality so laid back it seems off the wall

The most relaxed and mild-mannered cat in the world

Causes tension seekers to keep their toes curled

Some people can't stand to see purrfect happiness unfurled

The Rexed Main Coon Cat

Out of every two hundred kittens one Maine Coon is a Rex

They are considered exclusive and in no way a hex

We are learning to accept what's unique in our world

We don't shave off straight hair because it isn't curled

Uniqueness prevents us from stacking the deck

The Russian Blue Cat

Sometimes a name just isn't true

A fact true of the cat Russian Blue

He's Russian but not in a hurry

He's blue but there's no cause to worry

It's his fur not his mood that is blue

150 CAT JOKES

The Scottish Fold Cat

A month after it's born its ears downward fold

This unusual mutation makes then precious liked gold

Its round-headed appearance

Causes proud owner's endearance

And once they've had one their owners are sold

The Selkirk Rex Cat

First bred in the Selkirk Mountains of Wyoming

Its respect for humans keeps it from roaming

It has an incredibly shaggy rex coat

Much more like a sheep than a goat

A rare beauty well worth brushing and combing

HOME
SWEET
HOME

The Seychellois Cat

With a pale white base and splashes of color distinct

This demonstrative pussy will stare you down and not blink

Its head is wedge-shaped with predominant ears

Its eyes are baby blue but they seldom shed tears

And they only wear colored tails we think

Tail Sale
1 FOR $35
— OR —
2 FOR $50

The Siamese Cat

The most rumor-laden pussy cat to ever draw breath

Stealing one from Siam Royalty brought a sentence of death

This ritzy breed is now best known for its yowling

It can vocalize louder than seven wolves howling

Its noise would scare a ghost half to death

The Siberian Forest Cat

Considered the ancestral grandfather to all longhaired felines

This sturdy cat originated several dozen inheritance lines

Any cat that could survive winter in Siberia

Could probably live through a bomb and diphtheria

Russian weather will either kill you or establish long lifelines

NORWEGIAN FOREST CAT
PERSIAN CAT

The Singapura Cat

This little cutie is perhaps the smallest of all breeds

But this Singapore symbol inspires enthusiasm with its deeds

From its name we might infer

It can both sing and purr

And it can certainly fill a cat fancier's needs

The Sokoke Forest Cat

Described as an African Tabby with a wood-grain appearance

Perhaps some wild cat background explains its perseverance

Now being developed in Denmark this usual Tabby

Will converse if you like without being gabby

Its unique look should guarantee its future existence

The Sphynx Cat

While the historic legendary sphynx was inscrutable

This cat's nakedness is obviously indisputable

Its appearance is attacked or defended

It wears what nature intended

But to its owners his loving nature is irrefutable

The Spotted Mist Cat

An experimental breed developed in Australia

They'll probably please you and will seldom fail 'ya

These affectionate felines don't mind being kissed

They are easily spotted but hardly ever missed

Send your thank you letters to Sydney Australia

Dear Spottie,
Having
od time.
Wish you were here.
"Mist" You!
XOXO
To:
Spotted Mist Cat
Sydney, Australia

The Tonkinese Cat

This American hybrid is another Burmese/Siamese cross

With its near genius cat I.Q. it knows who's the boss

If you own a nice home they know just what to do

Mind your P's and your Q's and they'll let you live there too

If they should change owners they are sure it's your loss

WELCOME

The York Chocolate Cat

Many people think this cat got its name

From the chocolate-colored splotches on its tail and mane

But I trust my researcher who's as sly as a fox

When he says this cat eats Hershey bars by the box

But we won't knock these New Yorker's historical game

ERSHEY